History of America

IMMIGRANTS
TO AMERICA

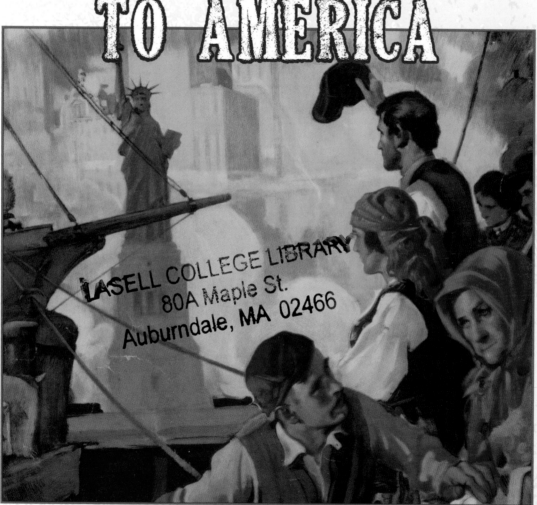

Written by **Linda Thompson**

Rourke
Educational Media

rourkeeducationalmedia.com

Scan for Related Titles
and Teacher Resources

www.rourkeeducationalmedia.com

PHOTO CREDITS: Cover, Title Page, Page 4, 6, 7, 8, 9, 10, 12, 13, 14, 15, 16, 17, 18, 20, 22, 23, 24, 25, 28, 29, 30, 31, 32, 33, 34, 35, 36, 38, 40, 41, 42, 43 : © Library of Congress; Page 13: © Fernando Regalado; Page 21: © Wikipedia, rudi wambach; Page 26: © Ron Chapple; Page 27: © Patrick Poendl; Page 37: © U.S. Department of Agriculture; Page 42, 43: © Wikipedia

Edited by Jill Sherman

Cover design by Nicola Stratford, bdpublishing.com

Interior layout by Tara Raymo

Library of Congress PCN Data

Thompson, Linda
 Immigrants to America / Linda Thompson.
 ISBN 978-1-62169-838-8 (hard cover)
 ISBN 978-1-62169-733-6 (soft cover)
 ISBN 978-1-62169-942-2 (e-Book)
 Library of Congress Control Number: 2013936387

Also Available as:

Rourke Educational Media
Printed in the United States of America,
North Mankato, Minnesota

TABLE OF CONTENTS

Chapter 1
AMERICA: A MELTING POT

Everyone in the United States of America is an immigrant or has descended from immigrants. This is true even of Native Americans, whose ancestors crossed a land bridge that once existed between Asia and Alaska more than 100 centuries ago. Pilgrims from England, conquistadors from Spain, **missionaries** from France, the Dutch colonists and the slaves they brought from Africa all came to America from somewhere else.

The ancestors of Native Americans crossed a landbridge from Russia to Alaska 15,000 years ago.

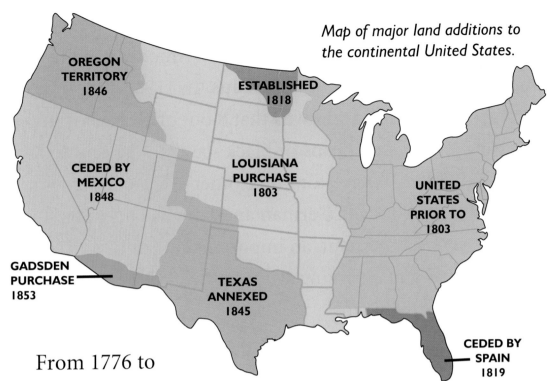

Map of major land additions to the continental United States.

OREGON TERRITORY 1846

ESTABLISHED 1818

CEDED BY MEXICO 1848

LOUISIANA PURCHASE 1803

UNITED STATES PRIOR TO 1803

GADSDEN PURCHASE 1853

TEXAS ANNEXED 1845

CEDED BY SPAIN 1819

From 1776 to 1853, the United States went from a cluster of 13 small colonies to what would become today's lower 48 states. As it grew, millions of people came to this vast new country from all over the world. People of every race and religion came, speaking hundreds of languages, bringing their labor and skills to help build a civilization. They built railroads, canals, bridges, sewers, ports, and subways. They worked as **tenant farmers**, producing food for the expanding nation, and many acquired their own farms. They worked in factories, sewing clothes and making machinery. Children born in the United States were citizens from the start, but their immigrant parents had to learn English and study hard to become citizens. And thousands of immigrants proudly fought in wars to defend their adopted land.

Before 1820, even with immigration, America's white population was largely **homogeneous**. In 1790 the United States took a census. It showed that 8 out of 10 Americans, not counting Native Americans or black slaves in the South, had English or Scottish ancestors. The other 20 percent of white Americans were mostly German and Dutch. This population was 98 percent Protestant, an important clue to U.S. citizens' overall values and emerging attitudes toward the waves of people who arrived later.

After the Revolution, the first great surge of immigrants to the United States arrived between 1820 and 1860. Almost every one of these people came from Ireland, England, Germany, Sweden, Norway, and Denmark. These are neighboring countries in Europe and the inflow of people did not change the primarily Anglo-Protestant make-up of America, even though many Irish and German immigrants were Catholic.

Early colonists left England hoping to find new opportunities in America.

At this time in the United States, plans to construct hundreds of miles of roads and canals and thousands of miles of railroads had created an urgent demand for laborers. Immigration increased

Chinese laborers working on the transcontinental railroad used explosives to blast through the mountains of the American west.

from about 129,000 people during the 1820s to 2,814,554 during the 1850s, more than a 20-fold increase. The U.S. population grew from 23.2 million in 1850 to 31.5 million in 1860, with immigrants making up a third of the additional people. Nearly half of those arriving in the 1840s and 1850s were Irish and more than a quarter were German.

The transcontinental railroad was built by the hands of European and Chinese immigrants from 1863 to 1869.

Immigrants typically spent their long sea voyage in a dark cargo hold.

The nationality of immigrants shifted dramatically between 1880 and 1890. By the turn of the century, most people were coming from Italy, Russia, Spain, Poland, Austria-Hungary, and Balkan countries such as Greece, Romania, and Yugoslavia. Part of this change had to do with the introduction of steam-powered ships. Immigrants typically traveled in the cargo compartment, or hold, of a ship delivering trade goods. Only northern and western European countries had large-scale trade relationships with the United States during the era of wind-driven sailing ships. These ships took bulky agricultural cargoes to Europe and returned with smaller cargoes of manufactured goods, so there was extra space for people in the hold.

THE APPALLING CONDITIONS ON BOARD

Early immigrants had to bring their own food, and some were near starvation or had died before the ship arrived in America. Each person had a shelf to sleep on, about 3-feet (.9-meter) wide by 6-feet (1.83-meter) long, stacked only 2-feet (.61-meter) apart. Poor ventilation and bad drinking water caused many deaths from disease. In 1847 about 40,000 people, 20 percent of those making the trip, died during the voyage.

When steamships became common, voyages between Europe and America took only 10 days, compared with the 30- to 90-day journey on a sailing ship. Now, ships could be devoted solely to carrying passengers, and the passage became affordable for peasants from poorer regions. In 1882, 87 percent of immigrants to the United States were from northern and western Europe. Only 25 years later, in 1907, 81 percent of immigrants came from eastern and southern Europe.

By the early 1900s, steamships had replaced sailing ships for ocean voyages.

The peak decade for immigration was from 1900 to 1910. During that period, more than six million Italians, Russian Jews, Hungarians, and other people from southern and eastern Europe arrived, making up more than 70 percent of immigrants. Americans felt uncomfortable with these new arrivals, who did not share their languages, skin color, customs, and religion. Citizens began pressuring their government representatives to restrict immigration. But immigrants flowed into the country in increasing numbers until 1924, when a tough law was passed that effectively halted immigration from southern and eastern Europe.

In the 1780s, a French immigrant named J. Hector St. John de Crevecoeur proposed that the United States should become "a melting pot." He said individuals of all nations are melted into a new race of man, who would be a mixture of English, Scotch, Irish, French, Dutch, Germans, and Swedes. This new man would leave behind all prejudices and traditions and be open to new ways of thinking and acting toward others.

In 1908, an English playwright, Israel Zangwill, extended Crevecoeur's idea to include the later wave of immigrants from the Middle East and the Mediterranean as well. Zangwill's play, *The Melting Pot*, was widely discussed across the country. It suggested the possibility of harmony among the very different peoples who were migrating to America. They would create not only a new race through **intermarriage**, but also a new culture by blending many ways of life into one. In the early twentieth century, such a concept seemed possible.

Since 1886, many immigrants were welcomed to the United States by the sight of the Statue of Liberty in New York Harbor.

Chapter 2
BEFORE THE REVOLUTION BEGAN

One of the earliest forms of immigration was unique to the United States and happened well before the American Revolution. Dutch colonists brought the first black African slaves, the only group of unwilling immigrants, to North America in 1619. By 1770 the colonies had about 1,600,000 people, of whom 21 percent were black. Most black slaves lived in the Deep South. This region was most suitable for growing cotton and slave labor was the most profitable way to grow large crops such as cotton and sugar.

In the early days of the United States, even the founding fathers owned slaves. George Washingon used slave labor to harvest grain at Mt. Vernon.

LIBERIA

After the American Revolution, African-Americans were not given full citizenship rights. Some Americans urged that free blacks return to Africa. This led to the creation of the Independent Republic of Liberia in 1847. President Abraham Lincoln told the first group of free blacks to visit the White House in 1862 that they should migrate to Africa. Eventually more than 11,000 African-Americans settled in Liberia.

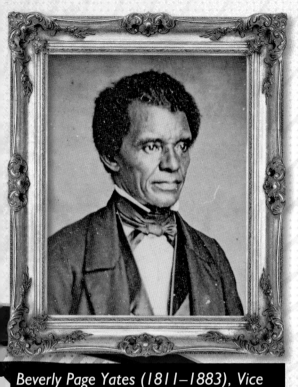

Beverly Page Yates (1811–1883), Vice President of Liberia from 1855-1859.

Also in 1619, a group of Africans were brought to Virginia where they worked as **indentured servants** and then became free. By 1790, about 60,000 free persons of color lived in the colonies, in the South as well as in the North. These Africans were in the same position as many poor white immigrants, who came as indentured servants. Whatever their color, indentured servants usually worked for a number of years without pay. Through their labor, they repaid the cost of their passage, which had been advanced by a wealthier colonist.

Immigrants traveled in covered wagons to reach new, unsettled parts of the United States.

More than 25 million Americans have descended from German immigrants. Although the country of Germany was not formed until 1871, people from Germanic states came to the New World in several waves. Political instability at home was usually the reason. By 1745 about 45,000 Germans and their descendants lived in Pennsylvania. They also tended to settle in frontier regions such as New York's Mohawk Valley, where they were often subject to Native American attacks.

These immigrants established Germantowns in Philadelphia and other parts of Pennsylvania in the seventeenth century. They became known as the Pennsylvania Dutch, although they were not from Holland. The name came from an American mispronunciation of *Deutsche*, which is German for "German."

German settlers were famous for crafts such as glass and paper making, publishing, tool-making, and beer brewing. They created the Conestoga wagon, which played a key role in settling the West. Germans tended to emigrate in groups, establishing communities such as Frankfort, Kentucky, and Fredericksburg, Texas. They maintained their culture and language in these communities, feeling less pressure to adopt the English language and customs than many other groups.

Scandinavians moved westward to Minnesota, Illinois, North and South Dakota, Nebraska, and Iowa. Many families migrated in a second phase to the Pacific Northwest. The great majority came from a farming background, and they sought work such as farming and mining in rural communities.

Scandinavians helped settle sparsely populated areas of the United States.

Chapter 3

A SECOND WAVE ARRIVES FROM EUROPE

The Irish began arriving in America in the 1820s. Like most immigrants to America, they came from the peasant farming class. Although they were free in Britain, they lived as if they were slaves in many ways. British landlords had taken most of their land and rented some of it back to Irish tenant farmers. As long as they lived in Britain, they had no hope of improving their station in life.

Irish peasants made their livings as tenant farmers.

Many Irish came to the United States because at home they suffered from famine, unemployment, and discrimination.

Beginning in the 1830s, a series of crop failures caused extreme suffering in Ireland. Between 1845 and 1855 a fungus made potatoes, the main food of the Irish, inedible. The resulting famine and related diseases caused more than a million deaths. Also, half a million people were evicted from their homes because of bankruptcy. During this period, more than 1.5 million people sailed for the United States.

The vast majority of Irish stayed in the northeastern United States. While the men went to work in construction, the women often became household servants. Nearly all of the Irish made their homes in cities, and American cities grew dramatically during this period. It was not only immigrants causing this growth, for general birth rates rose along with survival rates. By 1900, six United States cities, New York, Chicago, Philadelphia, St. Louis, Boston, and Baltimore had more than half a million residents.

From 1820 to 1880, the Irish made up more than a third of all U.S. immigrants.

Unlike the Irish and Italians, Jews did not work as servants. They arrived just as the ready-made clothing industry was getting underway. This development allowed everyone to wear new, instead of hand-me-down clothes for affordable prices. By 1885, there were 241 clothing factories in New York City. Eastern European Jews found work making and selling clothing for German Jewish owners.

Because of their love of education, Jewish people also rose quickly in the professions and in fields such as manufacturing, banking, the arts, and the entertainment industry. Despite the many obstacles they faced, millions fulfilled the rags to riches dream that every immigrant had upon arriving in America.

Albert Einstein (1879–1955) immigrated to America in 1933, becoming an American citizen in 1940.

SOME FAMOUS IMMIGRANTS

Millions of immigrants made valuable contributions in all kinds of fields. For example: Albert Einstein (German), Nobel Prize scientist, arrived in 1933. Irving Berlin (Russian), Broadway composer, arrived in 1893. Frank Capra (Italian), award-winning film director, arrived in 1903. Felix Frankfurter (Austria), U.S. Supreme Court justice, arrived in 1894. Knute Rockne (Norway), Notre Dame football coach, arrived in 1893. Maureen O'Hara (Ireland), award-winning actress, arrived in 1939.

Irving Berlin (1888–1989)

In the late nineteenth century, another large wave of immigrants arrived, this time from Italy. Before 1870, only about 26,000 Italians had come to the United States, and they were mostly northern Italians. Many became fruit merchants in the eastern states or helped establish the wine industry in California. But during the 1880s, much larger numbers began to arrive from southern Italy. By 1900 more than 100,000 southern Italians had passed through New York's **Ellis Island**, the federal immigration station.

Modern Italy was created in 1861 out of many regions that had been separated by mountains or the sea. The poorest and less fertile regions are in the south of the country. People from the south lagged behind other Italians in education, and most of them could not read or write. When they came to America, they came with the dream of earning money and returning to Italy. Nearly 90 percent were male. Those who remained in America almost always married someone from their own region of Italy.

Many Italian immigrants made a living selling fresh fruits and vegetables in cities, such as in Philadelphia's Italian Market area, which still operates today.

Immigrant laborers arrive in New York before continuing west to work in coal mines. Coal companies recruited immigrants and African-Americans to do the mining work.

In the United States they found work collecting garbage, selling rags, shining shoes, helping on fishing boats, and in construction. They became stonemasons, sailors, barbers, tailors, or shoemakers. The women tended not to work outside the home.

Many immigrants had signed contracts to work in mines or factories once they arrived in America. Italian immigrants were often indebted to *padroni* (self-appointed agents), who made a living bringing immigrant labor to America. The immigrant had to pay back the advances and loans, plus interest, out of his wages.

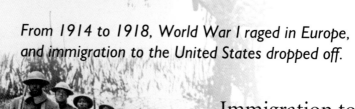
From 1914 to 1918, World War I raged in Europe, and immigration to the United States dropped off.

Immigration to the United States dropped during the Civil War from 1861 to 1865. It picked up and then fell sharply again in the mid-1890s because of an economic **depression** in America. Between 1900 and 1914, about a million immigrants a year entered the United States. This movement all but ceased during World War I and then soared again after 1918. But by this point, new restrictions on immigration made it harder.

IMMIGRATION LAWS

The United States had had an "open door" policy, but gradually it became more restricted. Federal laws passed in 1882 excluded people who might become a burden on the government. These included those who were handicapped, mentally ill, convicted criminals, or people thought unlikely to support themselves. Congress approved limits on immigration in 1921 and 1924, and introduced the idea of quotas. The 1924 law gave 82 percent of the openings to northern and western Europeans, and only 16 percent to southern and eastern Europeans. These quotas remained in place with minor changes until 1965.

Chapter 4

ARRIVING AT ELLIS ISLAND

As America's largest port city since the 1820s, New York received the largest share of immigrants. After 1892, essentially all Europeans came through Ellis Island, the first federal immigration station.

From 1855 to 1890, Castle Carden was America's official immigration center.

Before Ellis Island, most immigrants from the east had come through Castle Garden at the southern end of Manhattan. Constructed as a fort in 1807, Castle Garden became an amusement park, a concert hall, and in 1855 New York City's immigrant receiving center. Nine million immigrants passed through Castle Garden over the next 39 years.

From 1892 to 1954, more than 12 million immigrants entered the United States through Ellis Island.

Swindlers commonly overcharged immigrants for hotel rooms, rail tickets, and money exchange. Castle Garden was meant to improve that situation. However, once a person left the station, dozens of swindlers were waiting. Newspapers began to investigate the stories of abuse. In 1890 the federal government decided to take control of immigration and build a receiving station at Ellis Island in New York Bay.

Ellis Island had been a gunpowder storage site. The storage buildings became dormitories, the island was enlarged, and the shallow waters dredged so that large ships might enter. A reception hall, hospital, laundry, and utility plant were added, and Ellis Island opened on New Year's Day, 1892.

Through the years, Ellis Island has been enlarged from its original 3.3 acres to 27.5 acres. Today, it is a National Monument and is home to an immirgation museum.

THE STATUE OF LIBERTY'S WELCOME

The inscription on the base of the Statue of Liberty reads:

"Not like the brazen giant of Greek fame

With conquering limbs astride from land to land;

Here at our sea-washed, sunset gates shall stand

A mighty woman with a torch, whose flame

Is the imprisoned lightning, and her name

Mother of Exiles. From her beacon-hand

Glows worldwide welcome; her mild eyes command

The air-bridged harbor that twin cities frame,

'Keep, ancient lands, your storied pomp!' cries she

with silent lips. 'Give me your tired, your poor,

Your huddled masses, yearning to breathe free,

The wretched refuse of your teeming shore,

Send these, the homeless, tempest-tossed to me,

I lift my lamp beside the golden door!'"

The New Colossus *written in 1883
by Emma Lazarus (1849–1887),
daughter of Spanish-Jewish immigrants*

The Statue of Liberty

From among several hundred people waiting on three large ships in the bay, a 15-year-old Irish girl named Annie Moore was chosen to be the first person to enter the new station. As she checked in, she received a ten-dollar gold piece, the largest amount of money she had ever seen. That year, 445,897 immigrants passed through Ellis Island. They filed into a giant hall, then inched through a maze of aisles until they reached the registry desk. Some failed to pass an inspection and were herded into wire pens.

More than 12 million immigrants passed through Ellis Island. Over one million people arrived in a single year, 1907. Such large waves of immigrants caused a backlash in American cities. Pressure quickly grew for restrictions on immigration. People resented that immigrants were willing to work for low wages. Some believed these newcomers might embrace dangerous ideas such as socialism, or cause labor disturbances.

Immigrants arriving at Ellis Island were asked several questions including their name, occupation, and the amount of money carried.

In 1921 the first of several quota laws was passed. The government began requiring steamship companies to qualify immigrants on board their ships. Ship owners had to gather information, including each person's name, age, sex, marital status, occupation, nationality, last residence, destination, and whether the person could read and write. There were

Theodore Roosevelt (1858–1919)

also questions about the immigrant's health, finances, and any time spent in prison or in the **poorhouse**.

Corruption increased, however, and in 1901 a scandal erupted. Immigration inspectors had been selling false citizenship papers, letting immigrants bypass the lines. In September 1903, President Theodore Roosevelt made a surprise visit to the island. He found that a woman and four children had been kept for four months in a detention pen and had them immediately released.

Immigrants spent between two and five hours on Ellis Island waiting to be processed.

Although there were interpreters, the rush to get thousands of people through in a day often left little time for translating. Agents who did not understand or could not pronounce people's names wrote down whatever occurred to them. Sometimes days passed before a ship could unload its third-class passengers because of crowded conditions. One Dutch immigrant wrote, "We were shunted here and there, handled and mishandled, kicked about and torn apart, in a way no farmer would allow his cattle to be treated."

Ellis Island continued receiving immigrants until 1954, when it closed because of declining numbers. During World War II, it was converted to a detention center for foreigners in the United States with the same nationality as U.S. enemies; Germans, Japanese, Italians, Hungarians, Bulgarians, and Romanians. The buildings deteriorated until 1965, when Ellis Island became part of the Statue of Liberty National Monument.

THE PHYSICAL CHECKUP

Before 1911, immigrants had to climb a long stairway, and doctors watched for any sign of limping or other problems. If signs of disease or deformity were suspected, the doctors made notes. About 15 to 20 percent of immigrants were tagged for further inspection. One humiliating test was for **trachoma**, a disease that led to blindness. Doctors lifted eyelids of immigrants with a buttonhook or their fingers. Sometimes one member of a family, even a child, showed signs of trachoma and was sent home, with the rest of the family allowed to pass into the country.

Many immigrants who were ill were treated at Ellis Island Hospital.

Chapter 5
ARRIVALS FROM THE WEST AND SOUTH

Today, San Francisco's Chinatown is the largest community of Chinese people outside of Asia.

During the nineteenth century, immigrants also began coming to the New World from Asia. By 1880, 75,000 Chinese immigrants, nearly all men, had arrived in California. They came to work in the gold mines and, in the 1860s, to build the transcontinental railroad. They lived in the Chinatowns of San Francisco and other cities. They worked as cooks and laundry men in the mining camps, domestic servants in the cities, and field workers. Many also worked in restaurants and grocery stores. About half of them returned to China.

The Chinese immigrants received very harsh treatment at the hands of Americans. Workers of other races were alarmed at this large supply of cheap labor. Mobs of whites periodically burned their homes, killing the inhabitants. A Chinese Exclusion Act was passed in 1882 to end immigration from China, and additional laws prevented Chinese persons in America from becoming citizens.

In the early 1890s, thousands of Japanese people began pouring into Hawaii to work for growers of sugarcane and other crops. After the United States annexed Hawaii in 1898, Japanese workers could migrate to the United States. More than 100,000 arrived between 1900 and 1910. Like the Chinese immigrants, they planned to return home and thousands did so. Those who stayed saved their earnings and bought small farms.

Angel Island in San Francisco Bay.

ANGEL ISLAND

On the west coast, between 1910 and 1940, most immigrants entered the United States at Angel Island in San Francisco Bay. These immigrants included Australians and New Zealanders, Canadians, Mexicans, Central and South Americans, Russians, and Asians.

Americans based their attitudes toward Japanese people on prejudices they held against Chinese people, often speaking of both groups together as "the yellow peril." In 1908, President Theodore Roosevelt arranged a Gentlemen's Agreement with Japan, which gave the Japanese government the task of keeping its people out of the United States. They could still come by way of Mexico or Hawaii, but the prejudice in American cities made their lives difficult.

In 1913 California passed the Alien Land Law. It said that because Chinese and Japanese people could not be citizens, neither could they own land. It was eventually unsuccessful because of Constitutional protections.

Because Japanese immigration was banned, for several decades all Japanese American children were U.S. born.

PICTURE BRIDES

The Gentlemen's Agreement with Japan allowed the wives of Japanese men in the United States to join their husbands, and parents to join their children. In 1900 there were 24 Japanese men in America for every Japanese woman, but after 1910 the proportion was reduced to 7 to 1. Some Japanese brides were chosen in Japan by the man's parents, who sent the woman's picture to their son. If he accepted, the picture bride was married by **proxy** in Japan and then was allowed to enter the United States.

During the 1890s, people of Asian descent also began to emigrate. Like the Japanese immigrants, Filipino immigrants came to America by way of Hawaii. The Philippines was an unincorporated territory of the United States, and in 1935 Congress decided it would let the Philippines become independent within 10 years. Previously, more than 55,000 Filipinos had entered the United States but now the door closed, allowing only 50 immigrants per year into the country.

Filipinos remain a large immigrant group in America. Since 1979, over 40,000 immigrate to the United States each year.

Because of discrimination against dark-skinned people, Filipinos could work only in low paying agricultural jobs. Most of these immigrants were men without families. As foreigners, they were not eligible for assistance when they had no work. They gathered in sections of Los Angeles and Stockton, California, where they were very isolated and had no family life. After 1948, when a law prohibiting interracial marriages was repealed, Filipinos began to marry and raise families.

In the late nineteenth century, immigration also increased from the south. The railroads had reached New Mexico in 1879 and Arizona in 1880, bringing job opportunities. Mexican immigrants began to cross the border, both legally and illegally, to work on ranches and farms, in mines, and in railroad construction.

Texas, New Mexico, Arizona, Nevada, Utah, California, Colorado, and Wyoming were once part of the Mexican Republic.

Mexican laborers came to the United States to work on farms. Today, more immigrants come to America from Mexico than any other country.

Mexican immigration grew even faster in the early twentieth century, with nearly 50,000 people arriving from 1900 through 1910 and about 219,000 during the following 10 years. When the Immigration Act of 1924 was passed, restricting Asians, even more opportunities opened to Mexicans.

During an economic depression in Cuba in the mid-1880s, thousands of Cubans came to the United States. Some went to New York, but most settled in Florida. Cuban cigars were very popular, and in 1886 Cubans built the first cigar factory in Florida. Within 10 years more than 100 cigar factories had risen up in the state.

Chapter 6

IMMIGRATION CHANGES AMERICA

In spite of the United States' reputation as a melting pot and a nation of immigrants, U.S. citizens have been generally hostile to immigration. The various groups of people have not disappeared in a melting pot. As a result of immigration, however, the newcomers, existing Americans, and the country itself have been transformed.

As factories arose to mass-produce goods, huge numbers of workers were needed. These jobs prompted millions of people to leave their farms and move to town. In 1790, 97 out of 100 Americans lived in towns smaller than 8,000 people. But only 10 years later almost a third of the nation lived in cities of over 8,000, and across the United States there were more than 400 such cities.

Cities had pockets of extreme poverty and disease. Ghettos on the Lower East Side of New York City were overflowing. More than 30,000 people were squeezed into half a dozen city blocks!

Working high above the street, immigrants helped build steel-framed skyscrapers.

Most immigrants desperately needed work, and their willingness to work for very low wages fueled the backlash against them. When the country passed through a depression between 1837 and 1840, a common laborer's wages fell from a dollar a day to 75 cents or lower. U.S. born workers resented the **influx** of immigrants who would work for even less.

In the workplace, it was tempting to use poor immigrants as **strikebreakers**. At first it was the Irish, who were not allowed to join labor unions. Then the Italians arrived. They became the strikebreakers, and the Irish joined unions. As Italians arrived, they became the strikebreakers, and the Irish joined unions. In the 1830s cities began to see more strikes and even riots, with workers demanding better wages and conditions.

AMERICAN TRADITIONS WITH FOREIGN ROOTS

Some of the traditions that are considered most American came from other places:

Hamburgers and *frankfurters* – from Germany

Pizza and *spaghetti* – from Italy

Bagels – from Jewish tradition

Tacos and *enchiladas* – from Mexico

Chop suey and *chow mein* – Invented by Chinese immigrants for American tastes

SLUM ANGELS

Two women established immigrant assistance centers in the slums. Jane Addams founded Hull House in Chicago in 1889, and Lillian Wald created the Henry Street Settlement in New York in 1895. There, a widow whose husband had died in an industrial accident could learn about her rights against the employer. She could obtain childcare so she could go to work. People were given lessons in cooking, sewing, English, and citizenship.

Jane Addams (1860–1935)

A Supreme Court justice, Louis Brandeis, said in 1919 that the immigrant must adopt "the clothes, the manners, and the customs generally prevailing here… substitute for his mother tongue the English language," and must come "into complete harmony with our ideals and aspirations, and cooperate with us for their attainment." Schools, business people, and political leaders all worked to make this happen. Civic groups such as the YMCA organized classes to teach immigrants English.

More than half of today's Americans have descended from immigrants who arrived in the United States after 1790. About 900,000 immigrants still enter the United States every year, although various organizations continue to lobby to restrict foreigners. Another 300,000 enter the country illegally. Their main reason for coming has not changed: a dream of freedom and a better life.

The melting pot, once a popular image of how immigrants were expected to merge with society, turned out to be misleading. Although intermarriage is more widespread than it was in the 19th century, today people tend to celebrate differences and see cultural diversity as a sign of a healthy civilization. During more than three centuries, immigrants from all over the world have taken their place in American society, becoming productive and thriving citizens. In spite of the obstacles they faced and the pressure to conform to a universal model, many of these groups have also managed to preserve their own values and ethnic identity.

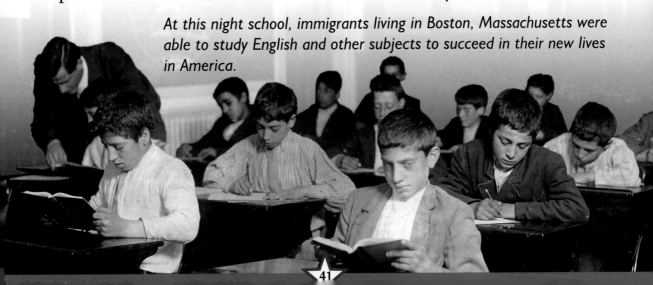

At this night school, immigrants living in Boston, Massachusetts were able to study English and other subjects to succeed in their new lives in America.

BIOGRAPHIES

Many people played important roles throughout this time period. Learn more about them in the Biographies section.

Crevecoeur, J. Hector St. John de (1735-1813) - French-American author who wrote about life in the New World. He published *Letters from an American Farmer* in 1782.

Brandeis, Louis (1856-1941) - U.S. lawyer appointed to the Supreme Court in 1916. In 1919, he stated that immigrants should learn English and live in harmony with the ideals of their new land.

Sullivan, Louis (1856-1924) - U.S. architect who pioneered the first skyscrapers in Chicago.

Roosevelt, Theodore (1858-1919) - 26th President of the United States.

Addams, Jane (1860-1935) - U.S. social reformer who co-founded Hull House in 1889, a community center for the poor in Chicago. Co-recipient of the Nobel Peace Prize, 1931.

Zangwill, Israel (1864-1926) - English writer, considered the founder of modern British-Jewish literature. His play, *The Melting Pot*, was the hit of New York's 1908 theater season.

Wald, Lillian (1867-1940) - New York nurse who founded the Henry Street Settlement for poor immigrants on the Lower East Side.

TIMELINE

1619
Dutch colonists bring the first black African slaves to North America, and the English bring the first free black African immigrants to Virginia.

1815
The first large wave of immigration begins.

1875
The first act to exclude people bars convicts, prostitutes, and Chinese contract laborers from entry into the United States.

1882
A Chinese Exclusion Law is passed.

1892
Ellis Island opens.

1921
The Quota Act sets an annual immigration limit at 358,000 and specifies quotas for nationalities. Only three percent of the numbers of any nationality in the United States in 1910 can enter per year.

1965
The Immigration Act is amended, abolishing nationality quotas and establishing an overall ceiling of 170,000 people from the eastern hemisphere and 120,000 from the western hemisphere.

1980
The annual ceiling is lowered to 270,000, and a system for handling refugees separately is approved.

1990
The annual immigration ceiling is raised to 700,000, but after 1994 drops to 675,000 a year.

1790
The first naturalization rule gives immigrants wishing to become U.S. citizens a two-year residency period.

1820s
Irish immigrants begin arriving in the United States.

1880s
Large numbers of eastern European Jews and southern Italians begin to arrive.

1891
The Office of Immigration is created. Today, this is the Immigration and Naturalization Service.

1900-1910
The peak decade for immigration to the United States.

1952
The Immigration and Naturalization Act combines past laws governing immigration and naturalization.

1978
A new annual ceiling of 290,000 replaces the separate ceilings for the two hemispheres.

1986
An Immigration Reform and Control Act raises the annual ceiling to 540,000.

Immigration to the United States, 1820-1970

Learn where immigrants settled when they made the brave voyage to the United States.

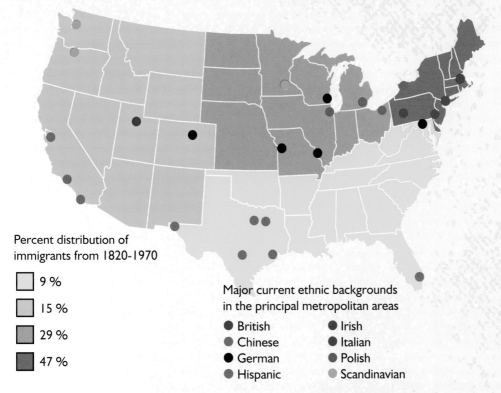

Percent distribution of immigrants from 1820-1970

- 9 %
- 15 %
- 29 %
- 47 %

Major current ethnic backgrounds in the principal metropolitan areas

- British
- Chinese
- German
- Hispanic
- Irish
- Italian
- Polish
- Scandinavian

Immigrants in the United States

This graph shows, by decade, the total number of legal immigrants who came to the United States.

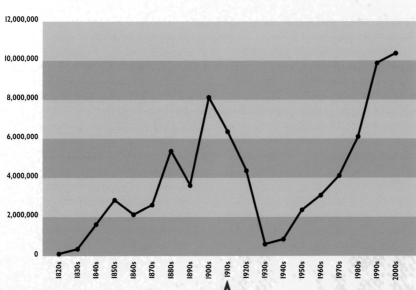

WEBSITES TO VISIT

www.besthistorysites.net/index.php/american-history/immigration

teacher.scholastic.com/activities/immigration/index.htm

ethemes.missouri.edu/themes/257

SHOW WHAT YOU KNOW

1. How many immigrants passed through Ellis Island?

2. Who are some famous immigrants who came to America?

3. Why was America called a melting pot?

4. Was it easy for immigrants to find jobs in America?

5. When did the first large wave of immigration begin?

GLOSSARY

anti-Semitism (AN-ti sim-uh-tiz-uhm): hostility toward Jews as a religious or ethnic group

depression (di-PRESH-uhn): a period of low economic activity and high unemployment

Ellis Island (ell-is I-land): an island in New York Harbor that served as the chief U.S. immigration station, from 1892 until it was abandoned in 1954

homogeneous (HOHM-o-jeen-ee-uhs): of uniform composition throughout

indentured servants (in-den-tyurd SUR-vuhnts): people who sign and are bound by a formal document to work for a specified period in exchange for travel expenses and maintenance

influx (IN-fluks): a flowing in of something, for example people

intermarriage (in-tur-MAR-ij): marriage between members of different groups

missionaries (MISH-uh-ner-ees): people undertaking a mission, especially a religious mission

poorhouse (poor-hous): a place maintained at public expense to shelter needy persons

proxy (prahk-SEE): authority or power to act for another

strikebreakers (strike-BRAY-kurs): people who are hired to replace a striking worker

swindlers (SWIND-luhrz): people who cheat others out of money or property

tenant farmers (ten-UHNT fahrm-uhrz): farmers who work land owned by another and pay rent either in cash or in shares of what the farm produces

trachoma (tra-KOH-muh): a contagious bacterial infection of the mucous membrane of the eye, which can result in blindness if not treated

INDEX